A Horse Calle

by Catherine Barr
Illustrated by Kristen Humphrey

Contents

OXFORD
UNIVERSITY PRESS

Meet Ed!

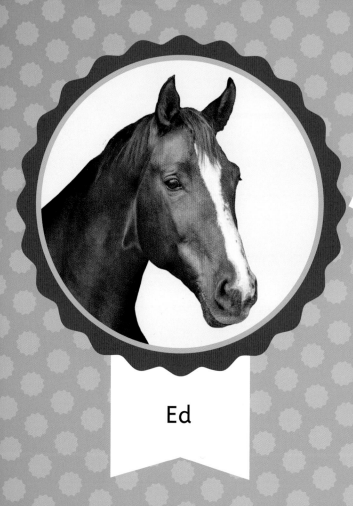

Ed

Ed is a large horse
with an important job.

I keep
people safe.

Ed is part of a team. His rider is an officer called Natalie. She looks after him, too.

We make a good team.

The stables

Ed lives in a stable. Here are some of the things Ed needs ...

Fudge

Ed

Ace

Judge

sign showing the name of the horse

Ed has lots of friends! They all live here with him. They do the same job as Ed.

Tacking up

Natalie brushes Ed every day. She checks him for injuries. She **inspects** his feet and cleans out his hooves.

brush

cleaning out hooves

When Natalie has finished grooming Ed, she puts on his **tack**.

Out on patrol

Natalie takes Ed into the city on **patrol**. Buses, cars and bicycles pass by. There is a lot of noise.

Ed is a very large horse. Everybody can see him on patrol.

Big crowds

Sometimes Natalie and Ed must go on patrol among big crowds of people. They keep watch and make sure everybody stays safe.

People might shout, cheer or dance. Ed knows not to get upset by this.

Time for school!

Sometimes, Ed will visit a school. He meets lots of children. They all love Ed!

Natalie tells the children what Ed has to do every day.

In training

Very few horses can do Ed's job. Ed is brave, quick to pick up new skills and well-behaved.

It took 2 years to get Ed ready to do his job. He had to get used to loud bangs, smoke and sheets of plastic that flap.

I trust Natalie to look after me.

Keeping healthy

A horse dentist visits Ed to keep his teeth healthy.
If Ed is ever unwell, Natalie will get a vet.

Another horse expert **trims** Ed's feet. Ed has to stand still while this is happening.

The end of a day

Natalie puts a rug on Ed at night so he is not cold. She gives him something to eat and drink.

Natalie will then write her notes for the day. She writes down what she and Ed have been doing.

Horse history

The Bow Street Horse Patrol was one of the first ever **mounted** patrols. Their job was to patrol the main roads in London.

This picture is from the 1800s.

Some horses have even been given medals for doing their jobs.

Olga, Upstart and Regal were given medals in April 1947.

These horses were brave when faced with danger.

Time to stop

When Ed is too old to do his job, he will stop and rest. He will spend his days in peace, munching grass and meeting new friends.

However, it's not time for Ed to stop just yet ...

Glossary

inspects	looks at something in detail
mounted	to have got on a horse in order to ride it
patrol	to go round a place to make sure all is well and people are safe
sign	a notice that tells people something
tack	the kit that you put on a horse so you can ride it
trims	cuts off the unwanted parts of something

Index

You can use the Glossary to look up the meanings of words that are in **bold** in this book. The Index will help you find key information.